Pablo Body Surfs

written and illustrated by
Tom Howard, M.D.

Pablo Surfs, a series

ISBN: 0615515568
ISBN-13: 9780615515564

To my surfer girls,
Love Dad

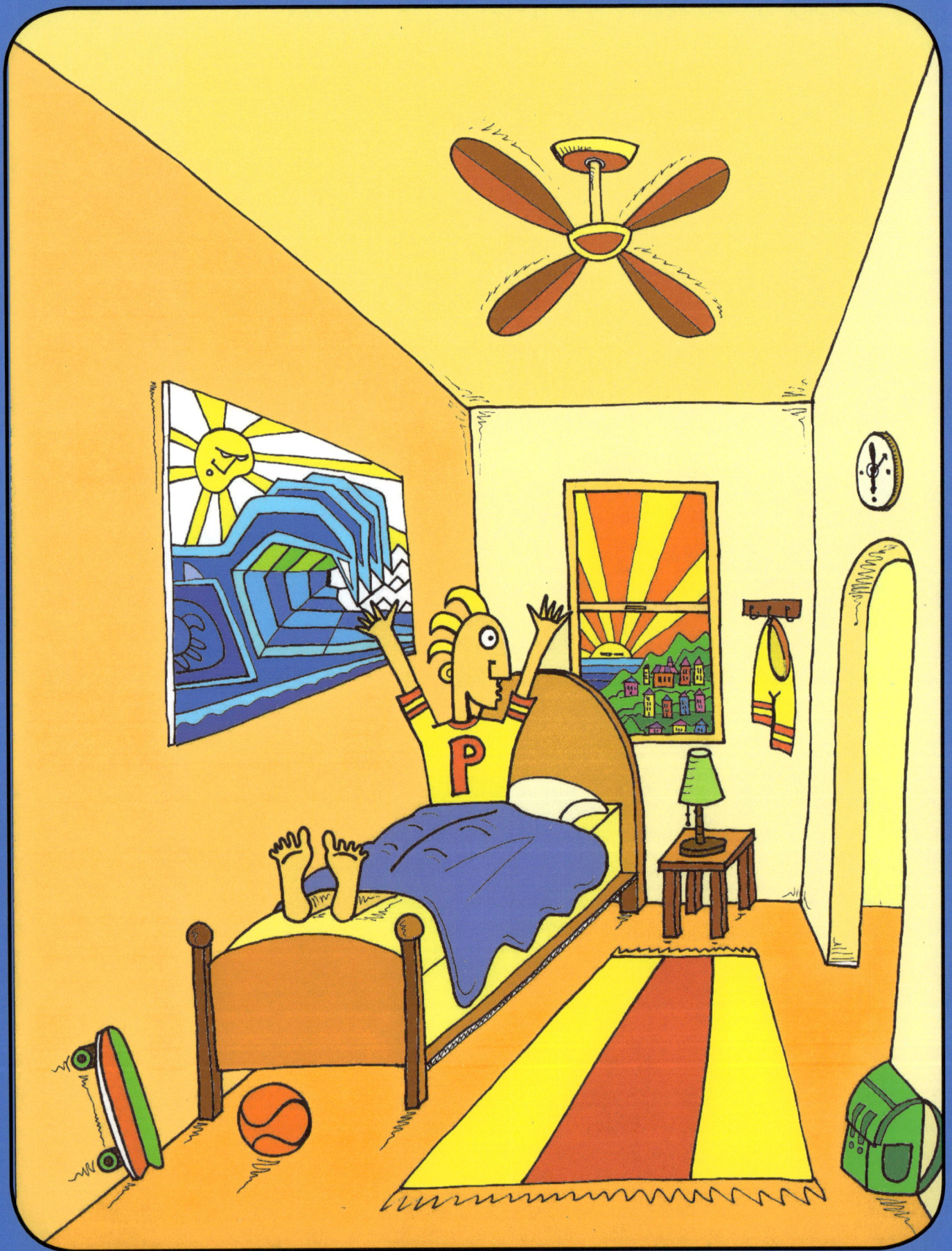

Pablo awakes with anticipation. He knows that today his friend, Mr. Jose, will teach him how to body surf. Pablo wanted to learn how to surf with a surfboard first, but Mr. Jose explained to Pablo that he must learn about the ocean and surfing the waves without having a board in the way. The surfboard would come later.

Pablo applies his sunscreen at home. Then he packs his backpack with water, food, extra sunscreen, a hat and his favorite towel. He jumps on his skateboard and cruises down to the beach to meet Mr. Jose.

2

Pablo gets to the beach, throws his pack down and
runs right down to the water with Mr. Jose.
"Pablo, wait wait!" shouts Mr. Jose but Pablo doesn't
hear him.

As soon as Pablo jumps into the ocean, a big wave comes and breaks right on top of Pablo's head. Pablo gets washed right back onto the beach.

Mr. Jose runs to see if Pablo is ok. Pablo is ok, but very
frustrated that the wave was so rough with him.
"Don't get frustrated, Pablo," says Mr. Jose. "I am going
to teach you all about the ocean and the waves."
This makes Pablo feel better.

"The ocean can be fun if a person has respect for it
at all times – the ocean is not a swimming pool," Mr.
Jose explains to Pablo. "The ocean is a beautiful living
ecosystem that is full of life and is ever changing."

Pablo and Mr. Jose sit by the water's edge. Mr. Jose teaches Pablo about the changing tides and how the current can change, moving in all different directions. Pablo learns that the wind's speed and direction affect the water. "Most important, Pablo, is to never swim or surf alone," says Mr. Jose. "You must always be with a buddy in the water."

Pablo is amazed to see how much there is to learn about the ocean. They sit together and watch how the waves break. They study the waves to see how many waves are in one set and which waves are the best ones to surf.

Pablo and Mr. Jose watch as a dolphin surfs in a wave. It is amazing to watch it surf so fast above and below the wave, always staying ahead of where the wave is breaking. This is called the curl.

Pablo watches the dolphin duck dive the oncoming
wave to get back outside.

Pablo and Mr. Jose soon realize that the waves are
breaking in sets of three and that the sets are coming
about five minutes apart. They are now ready to
carefully enter the water while always looking for sea
life. Mr. Jose shows Pablo how to shuffle his feet to
avoid stepping on a stingray hiding in the sand.

Mr. Jose teaches Pablo how to duck dive under the oncoming waves. They swim out together to a place just beyond the breaking waves. "Never turn your back on the ocean, Pablo, waves sometimes come in that you are not expecting," explains Mr. Jose. "As long as you and your buddy are watching for them, you will never be surprised." That makes sense to Pablo.

Mr. Jose teaches Pablo to pick two points on the beach to stay between. This is the best way to be in the right place where the waves are breaking best. Today it's between the lifeguard station and the public beach access.

They wait patiently for the next set of waves to come.
They already know that the first two waves of the set are
the best ones. They look out and see the waves coming.
Mr. Jose tells Pablo to start swimming as fast as he can
toward the beach to gain the speed he will need to catch
the wave. Pablo starts too late and the wave goes right by
him. Pablo gets frustrated but keeps trying. "I am proud
of you, Pablo, for trying so hard," Mr. Jose says.

Pablo tries many more times to catch a wave, but
they keep going right by him. He watches Mr. Jose
catch a wave. Mr. Jose glides down the face of
the wave effortlessly with one arm in front and
one toward the back to guide him. Pablo is now
determined to catch a wave just like Mr. Jose.

Pablo starts out for a wave, but realizes he is very
tired and hungry. "I need to take a break, Mr. Jose,"
says Pablo and together they swim back to shore.
Pablo and Mr. Jose make sure to drink plenty of
water and reapply their sunscreen. They have lunch
together and Mr. Jose says they must wait awhile
before going back in the ocean. As their food digests
from lunch, they can see that the tide is rising and
the waves are breaking even better than before.

Now they are ready to head back in and try again. They see the next set of waves coming in. Mr. Jose coaches Pablo to wait, wait, wait, and GO! "Start swimming, Pablo, as hard and fast as you can," says Mr. Jose. Pablo goes without hesitation, just like Mr. Jose did. Suddenly, he feels his body going faster and lifting up. He lifts his head and moves one arm in front of him and the other backward by his side. Pablo begins to glide down the face of the wave. It is effortless and fast.

Pablo is exhilarated! The wave continues to push him
forward and left, just ahead of the curl of the wave.
Pablo glides down the face of the wave all the way
to the beach. Mr. Jose is right behind him.

Pablo stands up in the shallow water, raises his hands in the air and shouts as loud as he can, "That was awesome!" He feels more elated than any other time he can remember. Mr. Jose gives Pablo a huge high five and tells him he is so proud to see what Pablo was able to accomplish today. Pablo now understands what "feeling stoked" really means.

Pablo and Mr. Jose catch a few more waves together
that day, but soon the tide is too high and the waves
stop breaking well enough to body surf. They swim
back to shore and pack up their belongings. As they
walk to the parking lot they pick up some garbage
that was left on the beach. They both know how
important it is to keep their beach beautiful.

"Thank you, Mr. Jose, for teaching me so much about the ocean," says Pablo. "I realize there is so much more to learn and I am happy to have a surfing buddy like you to teach me." Mr. Jose invites Pablo to body surf again next weekend. Pablo is so excited!

TNH 11'

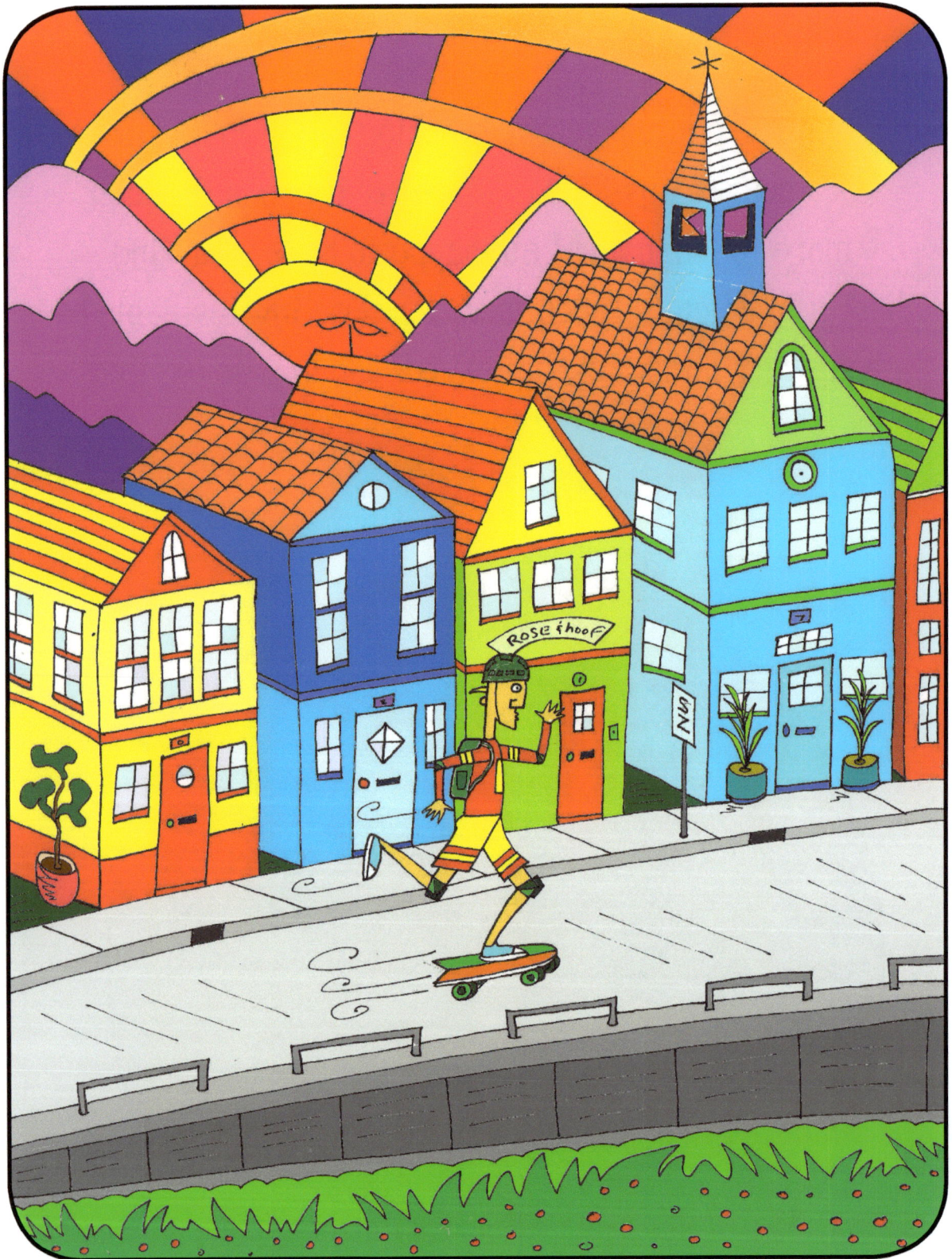

Pablo skates home feeling the "stoke" the entire way.

Pablo lies in bed that night, so tired, but still exhilarated from his day. He knows now that he will always be a surfer! Pablo sleeps well that night, dreaming about his next day of surfing.

About the author...

Dr. Tom Howard has been practicing medicine since 1999, but has always had a passion for surfing and drawing. He has combined these two loves to author and illustrate his first book, *Pablo Body Surfs*, the first story in the Pablo Surfs series. He wanted to create books that his girls would love to read. Dr. Howard lives in South Carolina with his wife and two daughters. Follow Pablo at Facebook.com/PabloSurfs.